INTRODUCTION TO

The Benefits
of the Bach
Flower Remedies

BY JANE EVANS

THE C. W. DANIEL COMPANY, LTD
1 Church Path, Saffron Waldon, Essex, England

First published in Great Britain by
THE C. W. DANIEL COMPANY LTD

SBN 85207 125 6

Reprinted 1977, 1979, 1984, 1987, 1989, 1991

DEDICATION

For

NORA & VICTOR

Printed and bound in the United Kingdom by Staples Printers Rochester Limited, Love Lane, Rochester, Kent.

A HEALER'S INVOCATION

Great Power of Powers, hearken ye,
Accept the joy Thou gavest me
And take it back
To magnify it thousandfold;
Then send it forth again
To where some sorrowing soul,
Or a hardened and embittered one,
Or one oppressed and burdened sorely,
Or another suffering anguish,
Severely tried by pain, has need of it.
Give it to them in rich abundance—
I shall not be bereft when it goes forth,
But glad to see it go,
For only by seeking to keep the joy
Close held and captured in my own small self,
Could it grow less and fade.

Take then the joy that Thou hast given,
And send it forth
Wheresoe'er Thou wilt.

Jane Evans.

BEFORE THE BEGINNING

"If only I'd known! All this could have been prevented." Words of regret, so often heard, so often spoken; and yet with knowledge comes the power of prevention. Prevention of illness should surely be the line of thought for advanced thinkers and advanced healers to help a progressive world make real progress and not merely change; change of medicine, change of treatment, shows change of attitude and some advancement, some desire to improve on old, accepted processes, but how far does that really represent progress, the progress towards the final elimination of disease, which is surely every healer's aim?

There is a system of medicine discovered some thirty years ago, though still relatively little known, whereby disease can be prevented before its physical symptoms are made manifest at all, the use of which involves very little cost. Perhaps that is why it is so little known. Accepting that the physical manifestation of disease is its final one, it is necessary to trace backwards and discover why and how it all began.

So often the final, obvious condition, one which may prove entirely incapacitating, is one which clearly cannot be ignored; frequent fainting, perhaps asthma, a heart condition, thrombosis even, each in its way representing some crisis. What causes the symptoms to exist at all? Why were these people so afflicted? What was the process that produced them? Not merely a physical lack which some neat little tablet can put right and all be well again, for that can only succeed in obscuring, obliterating the signs, and so making the true healer's task harder by producing a shadowy illusion and a false sense of security for the sufferer.

Dr. Bach advocated treating the **person** and not the symptom, and this is the way also that leads to prevention. The story of his discoveries is wonderful and very fascinating, and the more one considers and ponders the simplicity, the more right it all seems; as simple as breathing, as uncomplicated as the sequence of daylight and darkness. One breathes because one must, it is natural law, and daylight and darkness are as inevitable.

It was the functioning of certain natural laws which gave Dr. Bach his necessary clues—and they were in every sense given to him as and when the need arose —but that story has been told most competently and fully by Miss Nora Weeks in "THE MEDICAL DIS-COVERIES OF EDWARD BACH, PHYSICIAN" and published by THE C. W. DANIEL COMPANY LTD.

The Remedies, potentised flowers which have long-recognised healing qualities, incorporate in their preparation the four elements, earth, air, fire and water, utter simplicity. Earth, wherein the flowers grew, and on which the potentising bowl is placed, air which surrounds them during the potentising process, fire from the sun (for only on a clear and cloudless day can one potentise at all) and water, clear and clean from a well or spring, uncontaminated, to fill the clear glass bowl. It is as simple as dew forming on grass—and yet how few are the days when one gets the flowers and the weather to coincide! But when they do, and a successful potency has been obtained, what delight, and how clearly the water in the bowl sparkles with radiancy.

So is the preparation made to heal, not an asthma, or duodenal, or a thrombos, but to change a negative or uneasy state of mind to a positive and happy one, to banish the fear, to remove the anxiety or worry, to ease the nervous tension and irritability, to reassure the doubtful, to strengthen the exhausted, and give confidence to the over-diffident.

When considering the patient or the sufferer then, the adolescent girl perhaps, who may have alarming fainting fits and general lassitude, it is most probable that there may be no physical lack, but no interest in the examinations she is working for, or the present **seeming** uncongenial programme which must be **worked through**. With the help of Clematis, interest

6

will be aroused in immediate things, the situation dealt with, and the faintness overcome.

On tracing back the thrombosis patient's history, one could discover some frustration in past ambitions unfulfilled, whereby Wild Oat could remove the blockage caused by uncertainty and doubt, and allow free flow of ideas, ambitions and ideals. Yet it would not be necessarily the same state of frustration which could produce the same manifestations in another person. Or the complaint in another person could have been caused by fear perhaps, which Mimulus could banish.

Therefore it is necessary to trace the process back from breaking point to cause, and so repair the damage and be able to build up again. When it is possible to get behind the facade which the sufferer may have built up, and discover the conditions, some of them many and seeming complex, and find the fear, the jealousy, the worry, the tension which set the adverse process in motion, then can one move forward.

And having recognised that adverse and unhappy states of mind, or fearful and uneasy ones, produce disastrous effects, then surely, one becomes watchful of the signs and administers or is able to administer to oneself at the very earliest onset, the right strengthening or corrective Remedy; when worrying thoughts assail, White Chestnut; when depression, Mustard; for irritability, Impatiens—and so dispel the negative state of mind and restore harmony and even balance so that the potential disease need go no further. In the recognition of the need for help, and the thorough acquaintance of the right Remedy, lies the means of prevention, and prevention is possible for all who wish to know and save themselves much unnecessary suffering.

THE EFFECTS OF THE UNDISCERNED CAUSES

Far too frequently a minor ailment is misunderstood —not that it should be inferred that one should pander to trivial aches and pains to become a miserable neurotic, but to interpret their warning aright and to act accordingly. For so often small discomforts are meant as indications, and should be accepted as such. They are meant to make one pause and consider, and so to prevent further complications.

It is in this process too, that Bach Remedies can prove so valuable, for if the indications are heeded, and the appropriate Remedies used, no further ill health need follow. So the frequent occurrence of headaches, of nausea, of weariness and general lassitude due, not to physical disturbances only, but to deeper, more fundamental attitude or state of mind must be traced to their **real** cause and remedied. When the unhappy circumstances have been discovered, instead of accepting with resignation the conditions producing them, prescribe Wild Rose, which is the remedy for abject acceptance, and so produce a positive state of mind which is enabled to change the conditions and use them to one's advantage. Or perhaps indecision, or uncertainty are the real basic causes of the malady, then Scleranthus would help to resolve the situation.

But there are times when matters are not quite so ready to take shape so obviously, when, in the ultimate scheme of things there is meant to be further unfoldment of the pattern, and instead of producing an immediate clearance, as one might hopefully expect, a further symptom seems to manifest. This does not indicate the failure of the remedy, nor is it anything to become alarmed about, but rather it is an encouraging trend, for it indicates a changing condition, and usually an improvement, though this may often be misinterpreted, for it is only through a **complete** clearance that a real cure can be effected, and it is at this point that a person little acquainted with the Remedies and their workings might be most likely to give up, just when the real help of the kind most needed is having effect.

This manifestation of other symptoms is not a sign of worsening conditions, nor of failure, nor a wrong diagnosis, but a sign that the original condition has changed, perhaps been eliminated altogether, and that another, underlying and perhaps hidden by the more dominant one, has been disclosed, come to the surface and is asking to be dealt with.

In a case of a person suffering from rheumatism—a rigid, cold, tightened-up person, Rock Water was given, also Mustard, for there was depression and Mimulus for fear of the future. Soon she noticed that she began to move more easily and with less pain, there came also a sense of freedom and release as her outlook became less rigid and severe—but she complained of indigestion, saying that she was sure it was the Remedy, for she had not been subject to it before, and so insisted on giving up the Remedy. She refused to accept that the Remedy could not possibly have caused indigestion, and was quite unable to see that it was part of the process of clearing her of malady, that things were actually moving. This was very unfortunate, as she would have benefited by the addition of Rock Water in a few drops added to her bath, so that the question of indigestion could have been quite overcome, but she had resolved to give the Remedy no further trial and refused further help, which was a great pity. People so often fail to understand the workings of Bach Remedies and attribute to them the same effects which they have experienced from other medicines—which they have come to suspect and mistrust.

Now at this point indigestion had undoubtedly become manifest in the patient, but that was a good sign for it showed that as the rigidity which was producing the rheumatism was gradually being removed, another unhappy state of mind, anxiety, was becoming more apparent. It was anxiety for the future which she was keeping hidden by superficial cheerfulness, and Agrimony would have been indicated at this stage. Had she continued a little longer with the Rock Water, she would have probably been in a fit state to have dealt with the anxieties as they occurred.

9

It is a tendency among people to not persevere long enough. Because there may be no immediate and drastic change with the first bottle, then they are too inclined to say, "This is no more use than anything else!" How few people stop to think how long—often years—a condition has been gradually growing, and how unreasonable to expect it to disappear overnight; in fact it would be no good thing if it did disappear too soon, for that would be something of a shock to the person. A condition which has been gradual in growing should be gradual in its removal, in the pattern of Natural Law. A sudden change of condition merits a quick response, so Star of Bethlehem for shock usually produces a rapid adjustment to enable one to deal with bad news or the unexpected event. People so rarely consider that the human system which has become conditioned to a certain state would be happy or right with a sudden change.

So the person who has suffered from lack of confidence must be prepared to take Larch for some time, and gradually find himself able to do more and more with ease and to assume responsibility increasingly. Should this change take place too rapidly, the person concerned, too eagerly taking on more than he was ready for, too soon, might become exhausted and discouraged. So in some cases the slow process is the right one. It may be, too, that patience is one of the qualities necessary, and this will only be strengthened by the slower process.

One may observe that the action of drugs may be rapid, but are they always good, and **really** beneficial? How frequently does one hear of ill effects and side issues of a distressing and alarming nature! I cannot stress too emphatically that with Bach Remedies there can be no possible fear of this happening. They can never do any harm, and one is encouraged to treat oneself.

It is not always recovery from a disease which is in the inevitable pattern. It may be that the patient is not intended to recover very soon, and in these circumstances it is not due to the failure of the Remedy that they do not do so, but in cases of this kind, where perhaps a long illness must be endured for some specific purpose, with possibly much pain in order that certain lessons may be learnt which cannot be learnt in any other way, that Bach Remedies can produce a strengthening of qualities helpful to deal with these conditions, so that they can be met with fortitude and serenity—and the appropriate lessons learnt and the intended purpose be achieved.

It can be that illness of a quite severe and serious nature may be necessary for the patient to experience at that stage for his further development, and so to gain from it. Here too, Bach Remedies can assist enormously, for although at a certain stage the patient may be progressing satisfactorily, he may become discouraged and begin to get depressed by a slower rate of progress than he feels right, may perhaps begin to doubt if things are going as they should, and at this point Gentian can give him reassurance while strength is being gained and that point passed.

There can come a state of exhaustion during the course of an illness, of mental weariness, when although the patient struggles bravely and patiently to make progress, with unfailing courage, yet somehow he cannot help feeling weary of it. And here Oak is the Remedy to help him forward and give him strength to continue making efforts.

It sometimes happens that a necessary and unavoidable illness can take a curious trend. The cause of it may have been some blockage preventing the flow of vitality, perhaps some old resentment, some fear with roots in the past, some sense of injury, some grudge—and all the while this has been acting as a dam preventing the free flowing of perfect accord and well-being. So it will be that not until this has been removed will the patient feel completely well and at peace with all the world. But when whatever it was that was preventing the flow has been cleared and removed, replaced by positive attributes and harmony

11

restored, then will the true healing take place and become manifest in the physical body last of all. Often when ease of mind has been restored and a changed outlook and attitude taken place, patients will be aware of it even though the physical takes a little longer to respond. They know that "they are better in themselves", and often say as much.

So if Bach Remedies may not have prevented the onset of an illness when one expected them to, they have not necessarily failed, for with the correct use during the various phases of the disease and its individual requirements, the patient can derive the benefit which the experience was intended to convey, and certain weaknesses having been strengthened in the course of the illness, the patient can be helped to induce the state of mind which can deal with difficulties and overcome them. For it is not the difficulties which must be removed but the state of mind induced to use those difficulties for advancement and personal progress.

So for, "I need strength, courage, patience, tolerance, and etc." begin to be aware that Oak, Gentian, Impatiens, Holly—are all there for that very purpose, to add their attributes for your strengthening and your healing.

EMERGENCY AND CRISIS

The value of Bach Remedies cannot be over-estimated when dealing with an illness of a really serious nature, for when the inevitable outcome has been recognised and accepted then they can help the patient combat all phases of the disease, and although a cure may not be possible, much relief may be found by being able to deal with the various conditions as they occur.

Thus, for weariness of mind and body, Hornbeam could ease the strain; for fear of the illness itself, Mimulus; for indecision regarding what course to follow, Scleranthus; for hopelessness, Gorse; for depression, Mustard—and so on, so that even the most trying and painful of times can be assisted and met with serenity.

When it has been acknowledged that the illness is not one to be combated, or resented, but accepted for the lessons one can learn from it, for the advantages of character to be gained and resultant strengthening of weaknesses unlikely to occur unless tested in this way, then the whole approach becomes changed, and one learns to "go with the tide." Trying to suppress by opposing, by using stronger force when clearly acceptance is what is asked, only introduces further disharmony and confusion.

It is amazing how resolution and courage are strengthened to make endurance possible when dealing with inevitably fatal diseases. I have known even cancer to be endured with courage when assisted by Bach Remedies where drugs were refused. The right state of mind and utter conviction that one's course of action is the only one for oneself can, in faith and trust and acceptance, go far to help one to overcome. Then finally, although one may seem defeated and death inevitable, by higher, more spiritual standards, one is supreme. Death may have claimed the physical body because "the hour in time had come," but the higher self has not been defeated nor held in subjection.

In this way and by this means the true healing is able to take place and the essential Being of the person concerned enabled to be prepared to go on towards further achievement. By complete integrity and submission without resentment, by the choice of selection and with determination constantly re-inforced by the frequent and regular use of Bach Remedies, even such a disease as cancer can be endured to the end, and an end, helped by Bach Remedy, quite free from degradation. With the assistance of Rescue Remedy, Rock Rose removes the fear; Clematis the faintness; Impatiens the irritability; Chery Plum the deterioration of the mind, and Star of Bethlehem all sense of shock, so that the passing is quiet and serene.

In some cases too, where all that was asked has

been endured courageously and it seems obvious that it is only a matter of time, Rescue Remedy will give peace and courage during that time and aid the process surprisingly and mercifully. Sometimes when the patient is unconscious, a few drops of Rescue Remedy applied to the wrists and temples can help him to relax and so ease the most difficult time of all.

Then in accident or sudden emergency Rescue Remedy is of tremendous value in speeding and aiding recovery, again helping the patient to help himself to hasten the process. There come times frequently when dealing with children when Rescue Remedy comes promptly to one's aid. Suddenly while on a journey by car a child may say "I don't feel well!" and a little pause for air and exercise, with a drink to which a few drops of Rescue Remedy have been added can work wonders. It may be necessary to stop again from time to time and repeat the procedure, but at least a worse disaster can be averted. I have known one administration prove sufficient for a journey of some thirty miles, and not even be necessary to safeguard the return journey with a further dose, and for the child to say, with reassuring certainty, "I'm quite all right now," and to remain so.

Then there can be the sudden persistent attack of coughing, aggravated by bitter winter wind, so distressing for a child unable to control it, and the response to Rescue Remedy is wonderful. Or the sudden onset of sickness from some childish fear or worry of seeming enormous proportions which can disappear after Rescue Remedy has been given, and quite suddenly, after wondering which of the usual childish infectious ailments this may precede, the child may say brightly, "I'm all right now." Even if other symptoms should develop later, and measles or something similar manifest, Rescue Remedy will have prevented the panic at the first onset of the complaint, and particularly in whooping cough is it of value, when bouts of coughing can be alarming, it has a calming effect, and the attacks gradually lose their severity and the

14

patient is prepared and learns to deal with them, so that in the more tranquil condition which results the natural healing process has scope and can take place.

I have been asked if the use of Bach Remedies is a form of healing only for the more advanced among us who can accept this way of thought, but the response of children and animals who offer no opposition at all proves them the most satisfactory of patients since there is no doubt or query in their minds, and answers this question for us. It is the simplicity and harmony with Natural and Divine law which aids the natural healing process which is so ready to take place, and is in no way complicated.

Most of all Rescue Remedy is at its supreme best when an accident occurs and help is needed urgently and suddenly, then a few drops can make all the difference. It was while a long-distance coach, when backing into position, caught a woman's foot and pinioned her against a wall that its immediate effect was noticeable and remarkable. By skill and prompt action on the part of the driver a bad accident was averted, but the woman was given Rescue Remedy and very quickly had regained her composure and was able to say, "I'm quite all right. Don't worry." She was far less upset by the incident than the people who were witnessing it. There was **no** shock effect, and the healing process was enabled to commence immediately.

For the adolescent too, Remedies of one kind or another, according to the temperament and the need, can be most beneficial—far more helpful than the popular drugs for they are neither habit-forming nor harmful. So instead of the tension or anxiety or fear preceding an examination, or the despondency or doubt of success afterwards, the various Remedies can deal with these states and prevent other symptoms from developing. Indeed Bach Remedies could go far in helping with the problem of juvenile delinquency altogether if one regards the problem in terms of difficulties for the individual person to overcome. Here

15

is much scope. No claims of success are made, but it could be given a trial.

Times of emergency and crisis are times when not only the patient needs Rescue Remedy, but it is very beneficial too, for those who are helping the sick one, and so to fortify themselves against the distress which they must endure in watching the suffering of someone they care for. Over a long-term period other Remedies would be beneficial, according to the individual and particular need, but in time of immediate distress Rescue Remedy administrated to nurse as well as patient can help both, so that all eventualities can be met with serenity and the knowledge that on higher levels, all is well.

For it helps the patient a very great deal if those around are free from fear, and have quiet confidence, are calm and reassuring, free from strain, anxiety or irritability. It helps them also to know that their loved ones are being aided in the general stress. Out of consideration for all whom one contacts at such a time to keep one's composure goes far to lessen the emotional upset and is immeasurably helpful. In this way recovery and convalescence can be aided and many of the trying times averted—or if that was not the way the pattern was intended, the bereaved may be helped and strengthened greatly by Rescue Remedy, so that with Rock Rose for fear, Star of Bethlehem for shock, Impatiens for irritability, Clematis for weakness and fainting, and Cherry Plum to restore mental stability, one's equilibrium may be restored and confidence regained to enable one to deal with all that may be required at such a time.

THE WIDER SCHEME OF THINGS

It seems clear to me that through the wise, correct and discriminating use of Bach Remedies as a preventive as well as a curative way of dealing with illness it should be possible to produce a harmonious people freed from disease and that which produces disease— fear, apathy, mistrust, jealousy, tension and all negative states of mind. From this one is meant to infer that the Remedies are not a 'cure-all', no such claim has ever been made for them, and Dr. Bach had no intention that they should be accepted as the complete answer to all health problems, but they can do a tremendous amount to help all situations. They can prevent a great deal of **unnecessary** suffering, freeing so many people at present held within useless limitations.

From the increased awareness gained by the understanding of the workings of the Remedies—and of humanity itself and its maladies, and from the extra energy released, how much more could be achieved! Those who have potentised the Remedies and have watched the whole process, have participated in something very wonderful, for there in the clear glass bowl of sparkling fresh spring or well water where the flowers float in brilliant morning sun, one is aware of contact being made with Forces on a Higher Level, for there a remarkable radiation shines forth and one knows that some inexplicable process has taken place so that even to be beside it watching, is to be elevated above the mundane for awhile.

This is no mere flight of fancy or very pleasant fantasy, but capable of being submitted to scientific investigation—since in this day and age only that which has been investigated scientifically can be accepted as of any consequence. Solarised water alone is of recognised value in healing, but there is in the potentised flower preparation a quality which is admitted as being present, and is recognised as something which cannot be analysed or defined. That surely, is the life— the force which never yet has been measured, analysed or explained—but which is necessary for the restoration of health to a diseased person.

For surely there is the element of death in any disease—a little death of some part of a person (and here I really mean a **person,** not a body) so surely, the only means of certain restoration and complete cure is through re-introducing life, the right radiance of life to replace the damaged or injured portion. This no drug nor poison can achieve—nor any preparation that has not the necessary natural elements.

There is no substitute for the sun. There is no substitute for the flowers. They each come at the right time of the year when all is in accord for their use and one soon gets to know by the brilliance of the glow of perfection about them when they are ready for potentising. It is preferable to use fresh clear well or spring water, but sometimes only tap water is available. Distilled water is 'dead', and should not be used.

All this is simple—as it should be. No complicated machines are necessary, nor any amount of accurate measuring. The quantity does not matter, but the quality does. There is just as much benefit in terms of value in two drops as in the whole bowl full—and that is why a larger quantity than that prescribed can do no harm. In a critical condition frequent repetitions of the dose prove helpful, not larger quantities; they are merely wasteful.

So, to look ahead and see this wiser way of healing more accepted and in wider use should be to see also a wiser and more advanced species of mankind, better able to lead and guide the world progressively. Only when the right harmonies have been achieved within oneself, with Natural Law, and with others, can one expect a more advanced way of life. And then one can expect it, for in the natural sequence of things one is ready for advancement, and has proved that with increased clarity of vision on a small scale and with lesser things, mankind is ready to receive wider vision, and can handle increased power in the right way.

Having learnt to go in harmony with Natural Law and not to try to subdue or force it into misuse, then will man, with a sense of true well-being, know peace within himself, be able to radiate peace, will expect peace, and will know how to achieve and maintain it with perfect balance — through harmony and the sympathetic understanding of Natural Laws.

Peace thus gained should lead to the higher evolution of mankind.

> See that you trample not blessedness
>   Beneath your feet unheedingly;
> Regard the lowly flower,
>   Accept the gift it offers you,
> That exalted its blessing may become
>   A mighty benediction.

———————————